For more Cook books visit:

www.dorvilpublishing.com

Disclaimer

- Although the author and publisher have made every effort to ensure that the information in this book was correct at press time, the author and publisher do not assume and hereby disclaim any liability to any party for any loss, damage, or disruption caused by errors or omissions, whether such errors or omissions result from negligence, accident, or any other cause.

- Some names and identifying details have been changed to protect the privacy of individuals.

- This book is not intended as a substitute for the medical advice of physicians. The reader should regularly consult a physician in matters relating to his/her health and particularly with respect to any symptoms that may require diagnosis or medical attention.

- The information in this book is meant to supplement, not replace, proper (name your sport) training. Like any sport involving speed, equipment, balance and environmental factors, (this sport) poses some inherent risk. The authors and publisher advise readers to take full responsibility for their safety and know their limits. Before practicing the skills described in this book, be sure that your equipment is well maintained, and do not take risks beyond your level of experience, aptitude, training, and comfort level.

- I have tried to recreate events, locales and conversations from my memories of them. In order to maintain their anonymity in some instances I have changed the names of individuals and places, I may have changed some identifying characteristics and details such as physical properties, occupations and places of residence.

Table of Contents

Shrimp Rémoulade with Two Sauces

SHRIMP

Leafy tops from a bunch of celery
5 bay leaves
3 whole cloves
2 cloves garlic, peeled and crushed
1 large lemon, sliced
½ cup salt
3 lb. medium shrimp (25–30 count)

RED REMOULADE SAUCE

½ cup chili sauce (bottled) or ketchup, plus more to taste
½ cup Creole mustard, plus more to taste
1 Tbsp. paprika
½ tsp. salt
2 Tbsp. lemon juice
¼ tsp. Tabasco
½ tsp. minced garlic
1 cup olive oil
3 green onions, green part only, finely chopped

WHITE REMOULADE SAUCE

1 cup mayonnaise
½ cup Creole mustard

2 Tbsp. lemon juice
½ tsp. Tabasco Garlic Pepper Sauce
1 tsp. Worcestershire sauce
½ tsp. salt
3 green onions, green part only, finely chopped

1. Bring about a gallon of water to a boil in a large pot and add all of the shrimp ingredients except the shrimp. Boil the water for 15 minutes, then add the shrimp. Remove the pot from the heat immediately and allow the shrimp to steep for 4 minutes, or until the shell separates easily from the meat.

2. Drain the shrimp in a colander and set aside until cool enough to handle. Peel and devein the shrimp.

3. To make the red rémoulade sauce: Combine all the ingredients except the olive oil and green onions in a bowl. Add the oil a little at a time, stirring constantly, until all oil is absorbed. Taste the sauce and add more chili sauce or Creole mustard if needed. Stir in the green onions.

4. To make the white rémoulade sauce: Combine all the ingredients in a bowl and stir to blend.

5. Place the shrimp on a leaf of lettuce, sliced avocados, sliced tomatoes, or Belgian endive leaves. Drizzle half the shrimp with one sauce, half with the other. The sauces can also be served in pools for dipping. MAKES EIGHT APPETIZER PORTIONS OR SIX ENTREE SALADS.

Sautéed Crab Claws

1 stick (8 Tbsp.) butter
1 small head garlic, cloves separated, peeled and chopped
1 lb. blue crab fingers
1 tsp. salt-free Creole seasoning
¼ tsp. salt
¼ cup dry white wine
1 Tbsp. lemon juice
2 green onions, finely chopped
Toasted French bread crescents, for dipping

1. Melt the butter in a large skillet over medium heat. Add the garlic and sauté until fragrant.

2. Add the crab fingers and sprinkle with the Creole seasoning and salt. Shake the skillet to cook the crab fingers evenly.

3. After 2 minutes, mix the wine and lemon juice together, and pour into the skillet. Add the green onions. Shake the skillet to combine the ingredients and simmer for 2 minutes more. The sauce should have a somewhat creamy appearance.

4. Transfer the crab claws and all the sauce to a bowl and serve with toasted French bread crescents for dipping. SERVES FOUR.

Gnocchi with Crabmeat and Prosciutto

Salt, to taste
8 oz. potato gnocchi
1 Tbsp. butter
1½ Tbsp. chopped fresh shallots
4 oz. prosciutto, sliced into thin slivers
8 oz. whipping cream
Freshly ground black pepper to taste
8 oz. lump crabmeat
Cayenne, to taste

1. Bring a pot of salted water to a boil and cook the gnocchi until they're set but not mushy—about 4 minutes. Drain.

2. In a saucepan over medium heat, heat the butter till it bubbles, then add the shallots. Sauté until they just begin to brown, then add the prosciutto and cook another minute.

3. Add the cream and bring to a low boil. Lower the heat and reduce the cream for about 5 minutes. Add pepper to taste.

4. Add the crabmeat to the cream and agitate the pan to blend. Cook until the cream starts bubbling again. Add cayenne and salt to taste.

5. Add the gnocchi to the pan and toss with the sauce to distribute the ingredients. Serve hot on small plates as an appetizer or amuse-bouche. SERVES FOUR.

Crawfish and Corn Beignets

½ cup milk
½ cup water
5 Tbsp. salted butter
1¼ cups all-purpose flour
4 eggs
Vegetable oil, for frying
1 cup boiled crawfish tails, chopped coarsely
1 green onion, tender green parts only, very finely sliced
½ cup fresh corn kernels
Salt and freshly ground black pepper to taste
White rémoulade sauce (see Shrimp Rémoulade with Two Sauces, this page)

1. In a saucepan over medium-low heat, blend the milk with the water. Cut the butter into chunks and add it to the water. When the water comes to a boil, remove it from the heat.

2. Add the flour and stir it into the liquid with a wooden spoon until well blended. Return to low heat and continue to stir until the mixture pulls away from the sides of the pan.

3. Remove the pan from the heat and add 2 of the eggs, stirring quickly to blend into the batter. Stir in the other eggs, one at a time, and keep stirring until smooth and completely blended. Turn the batter out into a metal bowl to cool.

4. Heat the oil in a deep saucepan to 350 degrees F.

5. Combine the crawfish tail pieces, green onion, and corn in a bowl. Add pinches of salt and pepper and toss to distribute the ingredients equally.

6. When the batter is cool enough to handle, scoop up a heaping tablespoon and form it into a ball. Push your finger into its center to form a well. Put a scant teaspoon of the crawfish mixture into the well and close the ball up, working it with your fingers a little until some of the contents start poking out a little.

7. When you have 8 or 10 beignets made, start frying them. If they're close to round, you won't need to turn them. They take 6 to 8 minutes to fry to a medium brown. Serve as an appetizer with the white rémoulade sauce.SERVES EIGHT.

Oysters with Pepper Butter

SAUCE

2 oz. Louisiana hot sauce, such as Crystal Hot Sauce
1 tsp. lemon juice
2 Tbsp. dry white wine
1 stick (8 Tbsp.) butter, softened

OYSTERS

Vegetable oil, for frying
1½ cups flour
2 Tbsp. salt-free Creole seasoning
2 Tbsp. salt
36 fresh, shucked oysters

TOAST AND GARNISH

Thirty-six ½-inch-thick slices French bread, toasted and buttered
Crumbled crisp bacon, for garnish
½ cup blue cheese dressing, for dipping (see recipe, this page)

1. To make the sauce: Bring the liquid ingredients to a light boil in a small saucepan. Reduce by about a third.

2. Remove the pan from the heat. Whisk in the butter, a tablespoon or so at a time, until you have a creamy-looking orange sauce. Keep warm, but don't keep the pan on a continuous burner or the sauce may separate.

3. To make the oysters: Pour the oil into a Dutch oven to a depth of 2 inches. Heat over medium-high heat until the oil reaches 375 degrees F.

4. Combine the flour, Creole seasoning, and salt in a bowl, and mix with a fork. Toss the oysters in the mixture to coat, and shake off the excess flour.

5. Fry the oysters, in batches, until plump and light brown. Drain on paper towels.

6. Put an oyster on each piece of toast, drizzle on the sauce, and garnish with the bacon. Serve the dressing on the side for dipping. MAKES THIRTY-SIX PIECES.

Caviar on Savory Lost Bread

2 eggs
1 cup milk
Pinch of nutmeg
¼ tsp. salt
Pinch of ground white pepper
2 Tbsp. pureed white onion
Small French baguette, cut into ¾-inch-thick slices
Vegetable oil, for frying
¼ cup sour cream
2 Tbsp. finely chopped chives
4 oz. caviar

1. Blend the eggs, milk, nutmeg, salt, pepper, and pureed onion in a wide bowl. Soak the bread rounds until they're wet with the custard mixture all the way through but not falling apart.

2. In a large skillet, heat about ¼ inch of the oil until it shimmers at the surface. Fry the bread, in batches, until they are well browned on both sides, turning once. Drain on paper towels and keep warm.

3. Spread a little sour cream on each bread round. Sprinkle with chives and top with a generous spoonful of caviar. SERVES EIGHT.

Mushrooms and Foie Gras under Glass

4 oz. fresh foie gras, sliced into eight ¼-inch-thick pieces
Salt and freshly ground black pepper
1½ sticks (12 Tbsp.) butter
2 cups mushrooms, the more exotic the better, sliced about ¼ inch thick
2½ cups whole milk
¼ cup flour
⅓ cup dry sherry
Eight ½-inch-thick slices French bread, toasted

1. Sprinkle the foie gras slices with a little salt and pepper. Heat a large skillet over medium-high heat and sear the foie gras until lightly browned on both sides. Transfer to a plate and keep warm.

2. Return the skillet to medium-high heat, add 1 stick (8 Tbsp.) of the butter, and bring to a bubble. Add the mushrooms and cook until tender.

3. Meanwhile, make a thin béchamel. Heat the milk until warm but not steaming. In a saucepan, melt the remaining ½ stick (4 Tbsp.) of butter. Sprinkle in the flour and stir the mixture until it turns into a roux, about 2 minutes. Don't let it brown. Lower the heat and gradually whisk in the warm milk, stirring constantly until the sauce thickens.

4. Add the sherry to the mushrooms and bring to a boil until the alcohol has evaporated, about 2 minutes. Lower the heat to a simmer and stir in the béchamel. Add salt and pepper to taste and cook over very low heat, stirring lightly, until the sauce penetrates the mushrooms.

5. Place 2 slices of toast on each of 4 salad plates. Top each toast with a foie gras slice and pour about ½ cup of the mushroom mixture over each serving. SERVES FOUR.

Creole-Italian Pot Stickers

DUMPLINGS

1 lb. spicy Italian sausage, removed from casings, or ground pork
3 green onions, finely chopped
1 small can of water chestnuts, drained and chopped
2 Tbsp. soy sauce
1 tsp. Asian fish sauce
2 Tbsp. Chinese rice wine or dry white wine
1 cup fresh spinach, washed, cooked, and coarsely chopped
1 Tbsp. cornstarch mixed with 1 Tbsp. water.
2 eggs, beaten
1 package of round won-ton wrappers (about 40)
Vegetable oil, for frying

SAUCE

¼ cup soy sauce
2 Tbsp. Chinese red pepper oil
2 Tbsp. rice wine vinegar
2 large cloves garlic, minced
1 green onion, finely chopped

1. In a skillet, combine all the dumpling ingredients up to and including the wine. Sauté over medium heat, breaking up the sausage or ground pork as it cooks to prevent clumping. Cook until no longer pink. Pour off any excess fat.

2. Stir in the spinach, then the cornstarch-water mixture, and then, gradually, about two-thirds of the beaten egg. Remove the skillet from the heat, transfer the mixture to a bowl, and set aside to let the filling cool.

3. Separate a few won-ton wrappers and place them on a cutting board. Brush the remaining egg along the top margin of each wrapper. Spoon a scant teaspoon of the filling into the center, carefully fold the wrappers over the filling to create a half-

circle, and then press the edges together to seal. Place the finished dumplings on a platter and cover them with a damp cloth to keep them from drying out while you assemble the rest.

4. You can boil the dumplings in about an inch of simmering water, but steaming them over a simmering pot works better. In either case, cook only until the wrappers become translucent, about 2–3 minutes. At that point, the dumplings are ready to be eaten, but you can add further excitement with the "pot-sticking" trick.

5. Heat 1½ tablespoons of vegetable oil in a nonstick skillet over medium-high heat. Space out as many dumplings as the pan will hold and cook until they're crispy brown on one side. (This is when they'd start to stick to a regular pot.) Turn them to crisp the other side, then remove and keep warm. Add a little more oil between each batch and continue cooking until all are done.

6. Mix the sauce ingredients in a bowl. Serve the sauce on the side.MAKES FORTY DUMPLINGS.

French-fried Parsley

Vegetable oil, for frying (preferably used before, but clean)
2 bunches of curly-leaf parsley
1½ cups flour
2 Tbsp. salt-free Creole seasoning
1 Tbsp. salt
1 egg
1 cup milk

1. Pour the oil into a Dutch oven to a depth of 2 inches. Heat over medium-high heat until the temperature reaches 350 degrees F.

2. Wash the parsley well and shake dry. Trim off the bottom parts of the stems.

3. Combine the flour, Creole seasoning, and salt in a bowl, blending it with a fork. Whisk the egg and the milk together in a second, much larger bowl. Add the dry ingredients to the wet ingredients and whisk to make a thin batter. Add a little water, if necessary, to make the batter runny.

4. Toss the parsley in the batter to coat evenly. Shake off any excess batter.

5. Working in batches, carefully drop the parsley into the hot oil and fry until it just begins to brown, about a minute. Drain on paper towels and serve immediately. SERVES EIGHT.

you and your guests move on.

Crabmeat St. Francis

4 cups heavy whipping cream
2 cups crab stock (see recipe, this page)
¼ cup dry white wine
4 bay leaves
1½ sticks (12 Tbsp.) butter
1 large green onion, finely chopped
2 large cloves garlic, chopped
¼ cup chopped white onion
¾ cup hearts of celery, chopped
½ tsp. thyme
Generous pinch of celery seed
1¼ tsp. salt
¼ tsp. cayenne
¼ tsp. ground white pepper
½ cup flour
1 Tbsp. chopped flat-leaf parsley leaves
4 egg yolks
2 lb. fresh jumbo lump crabmeat
½ cup bread crumbs

1. Preheat the oven to 425 degrees F. In a saucepan, bring the cream, crab stock, wine, and bay leaves to a simmer and hold there.

2. Melt the butter in a medium skillet over medium heat. Add the remaining ingredients up to (but not including) the flour and sauté until the vegetables are translucent.

3. Make a blond roux by adding the flour to the vegetables and cook, stirring often, for about 5 minutes, or until the flour is no longer raw and just starting to brown.

4. Whisk in the cream-and-stock mixture. Lower the heat, add the parsley, and gently simmer for about 15 minutes. Remove and discard the bay leaves.

5. Remove the skillet from the heat and whisk in the egg yolks, one at a time.

6. Place 2 oz. of the lump crabmeat in each of 16 ramekins or baking shells. Top each with a ½ cup of the sauce, sprinkle lightly with the bread crumbs, and bake until the

top is browned and bubbly, 10–12 minutes.SERVES SIXTEEN.

Crabmeat Ravigote

½ cup mayonnaise
2 Tbsp. cider vinegar
1 Tbsp. Creole mustard
¼ cup heavy whipping cream
1 green onion, green parts only, finely chopped
3 sprigs flat-leaf parsley, leaves only, chopped
2 Tbsp. small capers, drained
½ tsp. dried dill
½ tsp. dried tarragon
⅛ tsp. salt
Pinch of ground white pepper
Dash of Tabasco
1 lb. fresh jumbo lump crabmeat

1. Whisk all of the ingredients except the crabmeat together in a bowl.

2. Gently stir the crabmeat into the sauce. It's best if you let the mixture sit for an hour or two, refrigerated, before serving. SERVES EIGHT.

Crabmeat West Indies

1 lb. fresh jumbo lump crabmeat
1 small white onion, chopped
½ cup olive oil
6 Tbsp. cider vinegar
1 Tbsp. small capers, drained
¼ cup water
¼ tsp. salt
4 dashes of Tabasco
2 ripe tomatoes, thickly sliced

Gently blend together all of the ingredients except the tomatoes in a non-metallic bowl. Cover and refrigerate for at least 2 hours or overnight. Serve cold over slices of ripe tomato. SERVES FOUR TO SIX.

Crabmeat Cannelloni

3 cups heavy whipping cream
½ cup grated Parmesan cheese
⅛ tsp. ground white pepper
½ tsp. chopped garlic
¼ tsp. salt
¼ tsp. crushed red pepper
1 lb. fresh jumbo lump crabmeat
1 Tbsp. fresh chopped basil
¼ cup shredded mozzarella

1. Preheat the oven to 400 degrees F. Cook the pasta in salted boiling water until al dente. Drain and set aside.

2. Boil the cream in a large saucepan and reduce by half. (Don't let it foam over.) Pour about two-thirds of the reduced cream into a skillet. To the cream remaining in the saucepan, whisk in the Parmesan cheese and white pepper to finish the sauce. Keep warm on the side.

3. Add the garlic, salt, crushed red pepper, and crabmeat to the cream in the skillet. Simmer over low heat, stirring until the crab is well incorporated. Add the basil and mozzarella, and stir very lightly until the cheese begins to melt. Remove from the heat.

4. Spoon about 3 tablespoons of the crab mixture onto the lower third of each pasta sheet. Roll them into tubes about an inch in diameter and place seam side down in a large baking dish. If using pasta tubes, spoon about 3 tablespoons of the crab mixture into the tubes. Spoon about 2 tablespoons of sauce over each cannelloni.

5. Bake the cannelloni until the sauce starts to bubble and the pasta edges brown lightly, 3–5 minutes. SERVES TWELVE AS AN APPETIZER OR SIX AS AN ENTREE.

Deviled Crab

1½ sticks (12 Tbsp.) butter
¼ cup chopped yellow onion
¼ cup chopped red bell pepper
¼ cup chopped celery
¼ cup dry white wine
1 Tbsp. lemon juice
1 tsp. yellow mustard
¼ tsp. Worcestershire sauce
¼ tsp. curry powder
1 lb. fresh jumbo lump crabmeat
3 Tbsp. chopped green onion
2 tsp. salt-free Creole seasoning
1 tsp. salt
1½ cups bread crumbs
2 lemons, cut into wedges
White rémoulade sauce (see Shrimp Rémoulade with Two Sauces, this page) or
   tartar sauce

1. Preheat the oven to 375 degrees F. Melt 1 stick (8 tablespoons) of the butter in a skillet until it bubbles. Add the onion, bell pepper, and celery, and sauté until soft.

2. Add the wine, lemon juice, yellow mustard, Worcestershire sauce, and curry powder, and bring to a boil, stirring to blend. When the liquid is reduced by half, add the crab, green onion, Creole seasoning, and salt. Stir gently, trying not to break up the lumps of crabmeat too much. Remove the skillet from the heat. Add the bread crumbs and gently stir until just mixed.

3. Although you can make the resulting mixture into cakes or balls (which you then bake on a pan in the oven, or even deep fry), I find it comes out better if you bake it inside clean crab shells or gratin dishes. Top each piece with about ½ a teaspoon of the remaining butter. Bake until the tops bubble and brown, 10–12 minutes

4. Serve with lemon wedges and white rémoulade sauce or tartar sauce. SERVES SIX TO EIGHT.

Oysters Rockefeller

4 dozen fresh, shucked oysters, with their liquor
2 cups chopped celery
2 cups chopped flat-leaf parsley leaves
1½ cups chopped green onion, green parts only
1 cup chopped fresh fennel
1 cup chopped watercress
½ tsp. chopped fresh garlic
3 anchovy fillets
¼ cup ketchup
1 Tbsp. Worcestershire sauce
1 tsp. sugar
1 tsp. salt
1 tsp. ground white pepper
½ tsp. cayenne
2 dashes of Peychaud's bitters (optional; see headnote)
2 drops of green food coloring (optional, but authentic)
2 sticks (16 Tbsp.) butter
1 cup flour
1½ cups very fine, fresh bread crumbs

1. Preheat the oven to 450 degrees F. Drain the oysters, reserving the liquor. Pour the oyster liquor into a 2-cup measuring cup, add enough cold water to make 2 cups, and set aside.

2. Working in small batches, process the vegetables and anchovies together in a food processor to a near-puree, using the oyster water to help things along.

3. Combine the vegetable puree and any remaining oyster water in a saucepan and cook over low heat, stirring occasionally, until the excess water has evaporated but the greens remain very moist. Stir in the ketchup, Worcestershire sauce, sugar, salt, pepper, cayenne, bitters, and food coloring.

4. Make a blond roux by heating the butter in a medium saucepan over mediumlow heat. Add the flour and cook, stirring often, until the mixture just begins to brown. Add the roux to the greens and stir until the sauce takes on a different, lighter texture. Then mix in the bread crumbs.

5. Place the oysters on individual half shells or in small ovenproof ramekins or gratin dishes. Top each oyster with a generous tablespoon (or more) of the sauce. Bake until the sauce just begins to brown, about 15 minutes. Serve immediately.

If you are using oyster shells, serve on a bed of rock salt or on a napkin to keep the shells from rocking. SERVES EIGHT.

Oysters Rockefeller Flan

OYSTERS

1 lb. fresh spinach, well washed, stems removed
1¼ tsp. salt
2 Tbsp. dry white wine
2 dozen fresh, shucked oysters, with their liquor
1 Tbsp. butter, softened
5 eggs
3 cups heavy whipping cream
2 Tbsp. Pernod
Pinch of nutmeg Pinch of ground white pepper

SAUCE

6 Tbsp. dry white wine
2 Tbsp. chopped shallots
1 cup heavy whipping cream
1 stick (8 Tbsp.) butter, melted
Juice of 1 lemon
Salt and ground white pepper to taste

1. Preheat the oven to 325 degrees F. Blanch the spinach for 1 minute in 2 quarts of boiling water seasoned with 1 teaspoon of the salt. Drain and douse the spinach with cold water. Drain again and set aside.

2. Bring the white wine and oyster liquor to a light boil in a medium skillet and poach the oysters in it for about 2 minutes. Remove from the heat, let the oysters cool a bit, and chop coarsely. Strain the poaching liquid and reserve.

3. Lightly grease the insides of six 6-ounce ramekins with the butter. Line the insides of these with leaves of cooked spinach, draping the ends of the leaves over the sides. Divide the chopped oysters among all the cups.

4. Whisk the poaching liquid, eggs, cream, Pernod, nutmeg, pepper, and remaining ¼ teaspoon of salt together in a bowl. Pour the mixture over the oysters in the cups. Fold the spinach leaves over the custard.

5. Arrange the ramekins in a large baking dish. Pour in enough hot water to come halfway up sides of ramekins. Bake until the custard is just set, about 40 minutes.

6. While the flans are baking, make the sauce. Boil the wine and shallots together in a saucepan until the wine is reduced to 1 tablespoon. Add the heavy whipping cream and reduce until sauce is thick enough to coat the back of a spoon. Whisk in the butter, lemon juice, and season to taste with salt and white pepper. Strain the sauce, discarding solids, and keep warm.

7. Allow the ramekins to cool for a few minutes after baking, then unmold onto serving plates. Spoon the sauce over the flans. SERVES SIX.

Oysters Bienville

4 dozen fresh, shucked large oysters, with their liquor
1 stick (8 Tbsp.) butter
1 lb. small shrimp (50 count), peeled, rinsed, and coarsely chopped
1 rib celery, coarsely chopped
1 large red bell pepper, seeded and coarsely chopped
½ lb. small white mushrooms, coarsely chopped
¼ cup dry sherry
4 strips lean bacon, fried crisp and crumbled
2 green onions, finely chopped
½ cup flour
⅔ cup milk, hot
2 egg yolks
⅔ cup finely shredded mozzarella cheese
1 cup bread crumbs
¼ cup grated Parmesan cheese
1 tsp. salt-free Creole seasoning
¼ tsp. salt

1. Preheat the oven to 450 degrees F. Drain the oysters, reserving the liquor. Put the oyster liquor into a 1-cup measuring cup and add enough water, if necessary, to make 1 cup liquid.

2. Heat 1 teaspoon of the butter in a medium skillet until it bubbles. Sauté the chopped shrimp until it just turns pink. Remove and set aside. Add 2 tablespoons of the butter to the skillet and heat until it bubbles. Add the celery, bell pepper, and mushrooms. Sauté until they get tender. Add the sherry and bring to a boil for about a minute.

3. Add the bacon, green onions, and reserved shrimp. Cook for another minute, then add the reserved oyster liquor. Bring the mixture to a boil and cook for about 2 minutes more. The sauce should be wet but not sloshy. Remove from heat.

4. Heat the remaining butter in a medium saucepan over medium-low heat. Add the flour and cook, stirring constantly, to make a blond roux. When you see the first hints of browning, remove from the heat and whisk in the milk to form a béchamel. (It will have the texture of mashed potatoes.) Add the egg yolks to the béchamel, stirring quickly to combine it before the eggs have a chance to set. Add the mozzarella slowly to the béchamel, stirring until the cheese melts.

5. Add the béchamel to the shrimp mixture in the skillet and stir to combine.

6. Mix the bread crumbs, Parmesan, Creole seasoning, and salt together in a bowl. Stir two-thirds of this mixture into the sauced shrimp. Set the remaining bread-crumb mixture aside.

7. Cover the bottom of a shallow baking dish with oysters, leaving just a little space between them. Top with the Bienville sauce. Sprinkle the top with the remaining bread-crumb mixture. Bake until the sauce is bubbling and the top is browned, 15–20 minutes (depending on the size of the baking dish). SERVES EIGHT TO TWELVE.

Creole-Italian Oysters

⅓ cup extra-virgin olive oil
24 fresh, shucked large oysters, partially drained
2 Tbsp. finely chopped garlic
2 Tbsp. chopped flat-leaf parsley leaves
1 Tbsp. fresh lemon juice
½ tsp. crushed red pepper
2 cups bread crumbs
⅔ cup grated Parmesan cheese
1 Tbsp. Italian seasoning

1. Preheat the oven to 400 degrees F. Pour a little of the olive oil into the bottom of a baking dish of almost any size, from a small gratin dish to a pie plate. Arrange the oysters in the dish, leaving about ½ inch of space between them.

2. Sprinkle the oysters with the garlic, parsley, lemon juice, and crushed red pepper. Combine the bread crumbs, Parmesan, and Italian seasoning in a bowl and sprinkle evenly over the oysters.

3. Bake until the sauce is bubbling and the bread crumbs on top brown, about 10–15 minutes (depending on the size of the baking dish). SERVES SIX.

Oysters Dunbar

2 dozen fresh, shucked oysters, with their liquor
2 Tbsp. salt, plus more to taste
Juice of 1 lemon
4 large artichokes
1 stick (8 Tbsp.) plus 2 Tbsp. butter
2 Tbsp. flour
¼ cup finely chopped green onion
1 cup sliced fresh mushrooms
¼ tsp. Tabasco
Freshly ground black pepper to taste
½ cup bread crumbs

1. Preheat the oven to 350 degrees F. Drain the oysters, reserving the liquor. Put the oyster liquor into a 1-cup measuring cup and add enough water, if necessary, to make 1 cup liquid.

2. Bring a large pot of water to a boil with the 2 tablespoons of salt and half the lemon juice. Cook the artichokes until tender, then remove from the water and set aside to cool.

3. Using a spoon, scrape the meat from the tough outer artichoke leaves into a bowl and discard the leaves. Pull off the tender inner leaves and reserve them whole. Remove the fuzzy "choke" from the artichoke bottom, chop the bottom into medium dice, and reserve.

4. In a skillet, melt the stick of butter until it bubbles. Add the flour and cook, stirring often, to form a loose blond roux. Add the green onion and cook until tender.

5. Add the reserved oyster liquor and mushrooms. Bring to a light boil, reduce heat to a simmer, and cook until the mushrooms are tender and the liquid is very thick. Add the oysters and cook for 2 minutes more. Season to taste with Tabasco, salt, and pepper.

6. Scatter the reserved artichoke leaves and meat evenly in a baking dish. Pour the sauced oyster mixture over the artichokes and top with bread crumbs. Dot the top with the remaining butter and bake until the bread crumbs are browned and the rapid bubbling of the liquid contents has begun to slow, 12–15 minutes. Allow to cool for

about 5 minutes. SERVES FOUR TO SIX.

Oysters Jaubert

1 quart fresh, shucked oysters, with their liquor
1½ sticks (12 Tbsp.) butter
1 medium onion, chopped
2 green onions, green parts only, finely chopped
½ very ripe green bell pepper, chopped
½ stalk celery, chopped
3 cloves garlic, chopped
2 Tbsp. Worcestershire sauce
1 Tbsp. Louisiana hot sauce, such as Crystal Hot Sauce
1 tsp. fresh lemon juice
1 Tbsp. salt-free Creole seasoning
½ tsp. salt
¼ cup flour
1 cup chicken stock, warm (see recipe, this page)

1. Drain the oysters, reserving the liquor. Put the oyster liquor into a 1-cup measuring cup and add enough water, if necessary, to make 1 cup liquid.

2. Melt the butter in a large skillet over medium heat until it bubbles. Sauté the vegetables until they turn tender, then add the oysters. Cook until the edges begin to curl, 3–4 minutes.

3. Add the Worcestershire sauce, hot sauce, lemon juice, Creole seasoning, and salt, bring to a boil, and hold there for about a minute.

4. Sprinkle the flour into the skillet and gently stir until the flour is fully incorporated into the sauce. This should make for a very thick mixture.

5. Warm the reserved oyster liquor in a small saucepan and gradually add it to the skillet. Add just enough warm chicken stock, again gradually, until the mixture has a stewlike consistency. Adjust seasonings and serve immediately over toast or pasta. SERVES EIGHT AS AN APPETIZER OR FOUR AS AN ENTREE.

Oysters Polo

2 sticks (1 cup) unsalted butter, melted
1 cup fresh bread crumbs
¾ cup grated Parmesan cheese, divided
1 Tbsp. herbes de Provence
Salt and freshly ground white pepper to taste
1 small onion, peeled
1 bay leaf
1 whole clove
2 cups milk
Few drops Tabasco (optional)
¾ stick (6 Tbsp.) unsalted butter
6 Tbsp. all-purpose flour
4 Tbsp. prepared horseradish, drained
Pinch grated nutmeg
24 fresh, shucked oysters, with their shells

1. In a bowl, combine the butter, bread crumbs, ½ cup of the Parmesan cheese, herbes de Provence, and a pinch of salt and pepper. Set aside.

2. Place the onion, bay leaf, clove, milk, and Tabasco in a small heavy saucepan over medium heat. When the mixture comes to a boil, remove the pan from the heat and strain. Reserve the liquid and keep warm.

3. Melt ½ stick butter in a medium sauté pan over low heat. When the butter is foamy, add the flour and make a blond roux. Remove from the heat when the first signs of browning appear. Whisk in the strained milk until the the sauce is fluffy and dry. Add the remaining ¼ cup of Parmesan cheese, horseradish, and nutmeg. Season with salt, pepper, and a few drops Tabasco sauce, to taste.

4. Fill a medium saucepan with water and bring to a boil. Fill a bowl with cold water and ice cubes. Poach the oysters in the boiling water until their edges curl. Remove with a slotted spoon and plunge immediately into the ice water to stop the cooking. Drain and set aside.

5. Preheat the oven to 375 degrees F. Place a layer of rock salt about ½ inch deep in 2 metal baking pans. Press half of the shells onto the salt. Spoon 1 tablespoon of sauce into each shell, then top with an oyster. Cover with 1 tablespoon more of sauce, then sprinkle the bread crumb mixture from step 1 on top. Bake for 10 minutes, or until a golden crust forms.SERVES FOUR TO SIX.

Oysters Roland

½ cup water
48 fresh, shucked medium oysters, with their shells
1 bunch curly-leaf parsley, bottom stems removed
3 cloves garlic
8 oz. small mushrooms, well washed
1 tsp. salt
1 tsp. freshly ground black pepper
Generous pinch nutmeg
1 lb. softened butter
1 cup French bread crumbs
French bread

1. Preheat oven to 400 degrees F.

2. Bring the water to a light boil in a small skillet. Add the oysters and poach for 2 minutes. Strain the pan contents, reserving oysters and liquid. Return the liquid to a light boil and reduce by about a third.

3. Put the parsley, garlic, mushrooms, salt, pepper, and nutmeg into a food processor, and process into a very fine mixture. Add the butter and process into a coarse, gritty puree.

4. Add the bread crumbs and the reserved stock from the oysters and process only long enough to mix everything thoroughly.

5. Place 6 oysters in the bottom of each of 8 small gratin dishes. With a spatula, lightly pack down enough sauce to cover the oysters completely, filling the dishes nearly to the top. (You can prepare the dish to this point and hold in the refrigerator. Take them out of the refrigerator a half-hour before the final baking.)

6. Bake the gratins of oysters until the tops are distinctly browned and crusty and the sauce is heaving and steaming. Serve immediately with hot French bread for getting up the extra sauce. MAKES EIGHT APPETIZERS.

Oysters au Poivre

2 dozen fresh oysters, the larger the better, preferably freshly shucked, with their liquor
2 cups heavy whipping cream
2 tsp. mixed dried peppercorns (black, white, green, pink)
8 sprigs fresh thyme
Pinch of saffron threads
¼ tsp. salt

1. Drain the oysters, reserving the liquor. Pour the oyster liquor into a 1-cup measuring cup and add enough water, if necessary, to make 1 cup liquid. Set oysters aside.

2. Combine the cream, peppercorns, 2 sprigs of the thyme, and the saffron in a stainless steel or porcelain 2-quart saucepan. Bring to a gentle simmer. (Watch to make sure the pan doesn't boil over, which cream likes to do.) Add the reserved oyster liquor and return to a simmer. Cook until the liquid is reduced to about 1 cup, about 30 minutes.

3. Add 6 oysters to the reduced sauce and let them cook until the sauce resumes bubbling, about 2–3 minutes. Using a slotted spoon or a skimmer, remove the oysters from the pan and keep warm while you cook the remaining oysters in batches of 6.

4. When all the oysters are cooked, plunge them back into the sauce for a few seconds to warm them back up. Arrange 3–6 oysters (depending on size) on plates. Spoon a little extra sauce over the oysters, stirring the pan to distribute the peppercorns and herbs. Garnish each plate with the remaining thyme sprigs. SERVES FOUR TO EIGHT.

Oysters en Brochette

2 sticks (16 Tbsp.) butter
Vegetable oil, for frying
1 cup flour
1 Tbsp. salt
½ tsp. salt-free Creole seasoning
4 dozen fresh, shucked large oysters, drained
12 slices bacon, each cut crosswise into quarters
Juice of ½ lemon
1 tsp. Worcestershire sauce

1. Melt the butter in a small saucepan over very low heat. Once the bubbles subside, skim the foam off the top. Keep the butter over the lowest possible heat on your stovetop.

2. Pour the oil into a deep, wide pan to a depth of about an inch. Heat over medium-high heat until temperature reaches 375 degrees F.

3. Meanwhile, combine the flour, salt, and Creole seasoning in a wide bowl.

4. Skewer the oysters and bacon on 8-inch-long metal or bamboo skewers, alternating each oyster with a square of bacon. Arrange them so they're barely touching. Coat the brochettes with the seasoned flour and shake off the excess.

5. Fry the brochettes, turning once, until the oysters are golden brown, about 2 minutes per side. Keep them warm while you cook the remaining brochettes.

6. Carefully add the lemon juice and Worcestershire sauce to the warm butter in the skillet. Careful! This may make the butter foam up again and perhaps splatter.

7. Use a fork to unskewer the brochettes onto serving plates. Stir the butter sauce to get some of the browned solids at the bottom and spoon about 2 tablespoons of the sauce over each brochette. MAKES EIGHT APPETIZERS.

Shrimp Limone

½ cup extra-virgin olive oil
2 cloves garlic, crushed
24 large shrimp (16–20 count), peeled and deveined
½ stick (4 Tbsp.) butter
¼ cup chopped shallots
10 sprigs flat-leaf parsley, leaves only, chopped
2 oz. lean, smoky ham, thinly sliced and cut into ribbons
½ cup dry white wine
¼ cup lemon juice
2 dashes of Tabasco
½ tsp. salt
8 thin slices French bread, toasted
8 thin slices lemon, for garnish

1. Heat the olive oil in a large skillet over medium heat until it shimmers. Add the garlic cloves and sauté until the garlic begins to brown. Remove and discard garlic.

2. Add the shrimp to the oil and sauté over medium-high heat until they just begin to turn pink. Add the butter, shallots, parsley, and ham, and cook until the shallots are soft.

3. Add the wine and lemon juice, season with the Tabasco and salt, and bring to a boil. Reduce the liquid by about two-thirds.

4. Place the French bread on individual plates. Place 3 shrimp on each slice and spoon the sauce over all. Garnish each serving with a lemon slice. SERVES EIGHT.

Shrimp with Fennel and Herbs

3 Tbsp. olive oil
1 lb. large shrimp (16–20 count), peeled and deveined
1 fennel bulb, finely sliced
2 cloves garlic, chopped
2 shallots, finely chopped
½ cup dry white wine
2 Tbsp. Herbsaint or Pernod
1 tsp. dried thyme
1 tsp. dried chervil
½ tsp. salt
¼ tsp. freshly ground black pepper
4 dashes of Tabasco
1 tsp. lemon juice
Chopped flat-leaf parsley, for garnish

1. Heat the oil in a skillet until it shimmers. Sauté the shrimp and fennel until the shrimp just begin to turn pink. Add the garlic, shallots, white wine, and Herbsaint or Pernod. Boil for about a minute.

2. Lower the heat to maintain a simmer. Add the thyme, chervil, salt, pepper, Tabasco, and lemon juice. Cook until the sauce thickens. Garnish with the parsley. SERVES SIX.

Spicy Garlic Shrimp

GARLIC MAYONNAISE

½ cup mayonnaise
2 Tbsp. Dijon or Creole mustard
1 Tbsp. red wine vinegar
2 Tbsp. chopped garlic

SHRIMP

¼ cup vegetable oil
1 Tbsp. chili powder
½ tsp. salt
¼ tsp. cayenne
1 tsp. chopped garlic
½ lb. small-to-medium shrimp, peeled and deveined
½ medium onion, sliced thinly
Four 2-inch squares Jalapeño-Cheese Cornbread (see recipe, this page)

1. To make the garlic mayonnaise: Whisk all of the ingredients together in a bowl. It's better to make this a day ahead of time and refrigerate to let the flavors blend.

2. To prepare the shrimp: Mix the oil, spices, and garlic together in a bowl. Add the shrimp and toss to coat. Cover and let marinate in the refrigerator for 1–2 hours.

3. Heat a medium skillet over medium-high heat. Add the shrimp, the marinade, and the onion, and cook until the shrimp are pink and firm, 4–5 minutes, depending on the size of the shrimp.

4. Split the cornbread squares and spread both halves with ¼ cup of the garlic mayonnaise. Put 2 cornbread halves on each of 4 plates and spoon the shrimp over the bread. SERVES FOUR.

Tasso Shrimp

6 Tbsp. butter, softened
Pinch of chopped garlic
Pinch of chopped shallots (or onion)
1 Tbsp. Louisiana hot sauce, such as Crystal Hot Sauce
1 tsp. heavy whipping cream
24 jumbo shrimp (20–25 count), peeled and deveined
4 oz. tasso, cut into matchstick-size pieces
Vegetable oil, for frying
1 cup flour
1 Tbsp. salt
¼ cup pepper jelly
Pickled okra or pickled green beans, for garnish

1. Melt 2 tablespoons of the butter in a medium skillet over medium-low heat. Sauté the garlic and shallots for a minute. Add the hot sauce and bring to a boil. Cook until very little liquid is left. Add the cream and cook about 1 minute more.

2. Remove from heat and gradually whisk in the remaining butter until it takes on a creamy consistency. (This is a New Orleans version of beurre blanc.) Keep warm.

3. Cut a slit down the back of each shrimp and insert a strip of tasso. Close the slit with a toothpick.

4. Pour the oil to a depth of ½ inch into a large, deep skillet and heat to about 375 degrees F. Meanwhile, mix the flour and salt together in a wide bowl. Dust the skewered shrimp with the seasoned flour. Fry the shrimp, in batches, until golden brown. Drain on paper towels.

5. Transfer the cooked shrimp to a bowl, add the sauce, and toss to coat.

6. Spread a thin film of pepper jelly on the bottom of each of 8 small dishes and arrange 3 shrimp on each plate. Garnish with pickled okra or pickled green beans. SERVES EIGHT.

Crawfish Boulettes

1 cup cooked crawfish tails, peeled
1 egg yolk
1 Tbsp. olive oil
1 tsp. chopped celery
1 tsp. chopped flat-leaf parsley leaves
1 tsp. chopped red bell pepper
1 tsp. chopped green onion tops
1 cup bread crumbs
1 cup flour
1 Tbsp. salt
1 Tbsp. salt-free Creole seasoning
Vegetable oil, for frying

1. Chop the crawfish tails very fine in a food processor. Add the egg yolk and process to blend.

2. Heat the olive oil in a medium skillet over medium heat. Add the celery, parsley, bell pepper, and green onion, and sauté until tender. Add the crawfish-egg mixture and warm through.

3. Add the bread crumbs a little at a time to stiffen the mixture. (You may not need all the bread crumbs.) Transfer the crawfish mixture to a bowl and set aside.

4. Mix the flour, salt, and Creole seasoning together in a wide bowl.

5. Pour the oil into a large, deep skillet to a depth of ½ inch and heat over medium-high heat until the temperature reaches 375 degrees F. Divide the crawfish mixture into 16 equal portions and shape them into balls. Roll them in the seasoned flour and shake off the excess. Fry until golden brown. Drain on paper towels.
   If you're serving this in Crawfish Bisque (see recipe, this page), drop 1–2 boulettes into each serving of bisque at the table or serve the boulettes on the side. MAKES ABOUT SIXTEEN BOULETTES.

Crawfish with Morel Mushrooms

1 oz. dried morel mushrooms (or 4 oz. fresh, if you're lucky enough to have them)
2 Tbsp. butter
1½ lb. fresh crawfish tails
1 Tbsp. chopped shallots
1 tsp. chopped fresh tarragon
1 tsp. chopped fresh chives
¼ tsp. salt
Pinch of cayenne
1½ cups cooked long-grain rice

1. Soak the morels in water to reconstitute them. Change the water several times to remove any sand.

2. Melt the butter in a large skillet. Add the crawfish meat and morels, and cook until they're hot all the way through—about 2 minutes. Add the shallots, tarragon, chives, salt, and cayenne, and cook for about 1 minute more.

3. Divide the rice among 8 plates and spoon the crawfish mixture over it.SERVES EIGHT.

Gratin of Crawfish Tails

MARINADE

¼ cup dry white wine
Juice of ½ lemon
2 dashes of Worcestershire sauce
1 tsp. yellow mustard
1 tsp. Tabasco Garlic Pepper Sauce

CRAWFISH

1½ cups cooked crawfish tails, peeled
½ stick (4 Tbsp.) butter

3 Tbsp. flour
1 tsp. minced garlic
2 Tbsp. brandy
1 cup half-and-half, warmed
½ tsp. dried tarragon
½ tsp. dried chervil
½ tsp. dried dill
½ tsp. salt
¼ tsp. ground white pepper
18 slices French bread, toasted

1. Preheat the oven to 400 degrees F. Whisk all of the marinade ingredients together in a bowl. Add the crawfish meat and toss to coat. Marinate for about 5 minutes.

2. Heat the butter in a medium saucepan over medium heat until it bubbles, then stir in the flour and cook, stirring constantly, to make a light roux. Cook until the texture changes, about 5 minutes, but don't allow the roux to brown.

3. Add the garlic and stir for about 30 seconds. Lower the heat to the lowest setting, stir in the brandy, and cook for about a minute. Add the half-and-half and whisk until the sauce thickens. Add all of the remaining ingredients except the French bread and simmer, stirring once or twice, for about 2 minutes.

4. Stir in the crawfish gently. Continue to simmer until the crawfish is heated through.

5. Divide the crawfish mixture among 4–6 ramekins or gratin dishes. Bake until the sauce begins to bubble and brown around the edges, 3–5 minutes. Serve immediately with the French bread. SERVES FOUR TO SIX.

Asparagus and Crawfish with Glazed Hollandaise

1 lb. asparagus, the tough bottom inch or two cut off
½ cup cooked crawfish tails, peeled
2 Tbsp. finely shredded Parmesan cheese
1 cup Hollandaise (see recipe, this page)
Cayenne

1. The best way to cook the asparagus is in a steamer, but it can also be done in a large skillet. If you're using a skillet, bring ½ inch of water to a slow boil and drop in the asparagus. Let the asparagus cook about 2 minutes, until crisptender, then remove, being careful not to break them. Run cold water over the asparagus to stop the cooking, then drain.

2. Preheat the broiler. Arrange the asparagus in a single layer, all parallel to one another, on a broiler pan. Sprinkle the crawfish and the Parmesan across the centers of the asparagus spears. Pour the hollandaise over the centers of the spears, leaving the tips clean.

3. Broil the asparagus until the hollandaise begins to turn light brown on top, about 3 minutes. Remove from the oven. Use a long metal spatula to transfer 6–10 spears at a time to a serving dish, making sure the topping stays intact. Sprinkle lightly with cayenne. SERVES EIGHT.

Seared Scallops with Artichokes

4 small whole artichokes

GARLIC BEURRE BLANC

½ cup dry white wine
1 Tbsp. white vinegar
1 Tbsp. heavy whipping cream
1 head garlic, roasted until semisoft
1½ sticks (12 Tbsp.) butter, softened
Salt and freshly ground black pepper to taste

SCALLOPS

¼ cup clarified butter (see recipe, this page)
1 lb. day-boat sea scallops, medium-large

VINAIGRETTE

1 Tbsp. balsamic vinegar
1 tsp. chopped fresh tarragon
1 Tbsp. chopped flat-leaf parsley leaves
1 tsp. grated Parmesan cheese
¼ cup extra-virgin olive oil

GARNISH

1 tomato, finely diced

1. Wash and then steam the artichokes until tender, 20–30 minutes. Pull off and save 24 perfect leaves. Clean and remove the artichoke bottoms and set aside.

2. To make the garlic beurre blanc: Bring the wine and vinegar to a boil in a medium skillet. Lower the heat to a low simmer and add the cream. Puree the roasted garlic with the side of a kitchen knife and add to the skillet. Whisk in the softened butter, a

little at a time, until the mixture takes on a creamy consistency. Add salt and pepper to taste. Remove from heat and reserve.

3. Heat 2 tablespoons of the clarified butter in a medium skillet over high heat. Add the sea scallops, in batches, and sauté until they are lightly browned but still bulging, about 1½ minutes per side. Add more butter to the skillet, as needed, to complete the cooking.

4. Combine all the vinaigrette ingredients except for the olive oil in a bowl. Gradually whisk in the oil.

5. Place an artichoke bottom on each of 4 plates. Surround each bottom with 8 artichoke leaves. Drizzle some of the vinaigrette over the artichokes. Divide the scallops among the 4 plates and spoon 2 tablespoons of the garlic beurre blanc over each. Garnish with the diced tomato.SERVES FOUR.

Chicken Livers with Bacon and Pepper Jelly

24 chicken livers
12 slices bacon
¼ cup pepper jelly
1 Tbsp. lemon juice
1 green onion, finely chopped
½ tsp. salt

1. Preheat the broiler. Bring a pot of water to a rolling boil.

2. Rinse the chicken livers. Cut the bacon strips, crosswise, in half. Cook the livers and bacon in the pot of boiling water for about 2 minutes. Remove, drain, and cool for a few minutes on paper towels. Roll the chicken livers and bacon on the paper towels to dry them.

3. Whisk the pepper jelly, lemon juice, green onion, and salt together in a small bowl. Roll the chicken livers in the pepper-jelly mixture to coat well. Place each liver atop a half-slice of bacon and roll it up. Skewer 4–6 bacon-wrapped livers together on metal or bamboo skewers, leaving about ½ inch between each liver.

4. Place the skewers on the broiler rack and broil until the bacon is crispy on one side, about 4 minutes. Turn and broil for another 3–4 minutes, or until the second side turns crispy.

5. Remove livers from skewers and serve, as is, as an appetizer. Or unload the skewers on top of red beans and rice for a unique alternative to sausage. SERVES FOUR TO SIX.

Natchitoches Spicy Meat Pies

FILLING

3 Tbsp. vegetable oil
2 Tbsp. flour
1 large onion, chopped
½ green bell pepper, chopped
1 lb. lean ground pork
1 lb. ground beef round
1 Tbsp. salt-free Creole seasoning (best: Bayou Bang)
½ tsp. salt
⅛ tsp. cayenne pepper
2 ribs celery, chopped
12 sprigs parsley, leaves only, chopped
1 clove garlic, chopped
1 tsp. Worcestershire sauce

CRUST

½ tsp. salt
4 cups self-rising flour
6 Tbsp. Crisco
2 egg yolks
1½ cups milk
2 quarts vegetable oil

1. Heat the oil and the flour together in a heavy, large skillet. Cook over medium heat, stirring constantly, to make a medium-brown roux. Add the onion when the color is right and sauté until the onion begins to brown slightly. Add the bell pepper. Cook for another minute.

2. Add the pork, beef, Creole seasoning, salt, and cayenne. Sauté, breaking it up as you go, until well browned. Pour off any rendered fat.

3. Lower the heat and add the celery, parsley, garlic, and Worcestershire sauce. Continue to cook for another 5 or 6 minutes, stirring now and then to keep anything from forming clumps.

4. Remove the meat mixture to a big metal pan to cool for a few minutes. Cover and refrigerate.

5. Crust: In a bowl, blend the salt into the flour, then cut in the Crisco and blend with a whisk till it disappears and makes the flour slightly crumbly.

6. Blend the egg yolks into the milk and add the milk mixture to the flour. Stir with a kitchen fork till mixed in, then with a rubber spatula to eliminate most of the dry flour. Stir as little as possible.

7. Dump the dough onto a clean, floured work surface and roll out about ¼ inch thick. Fold the dough into thirds, to make three layers. Roll out again, this time to the thickness of two stacked quarters. (This will make it pretty wide; you might want to cut it in half.) Cut out circles about 6 inches in diameter. Handling the dough as little as possible, roll out the leftover dough to cut another batch of circles.

8. Spoon about 3 tablespoons of the meat mixture onto one half of a dough circle. Moisten the edge of the circle with a little water. Fold the circle over into a half-moon and press down the edges with a fork to seal.

9. Heat the vegetable oil in a heavy, deep kettle to 350 degrees F. Fry no more than 2 pies at a time until golden brown. Let the heat of the oil recover between batches. MAKES EIGHTEEN TO TWENTY-FOUR PIES.

Frogs' Legs Persillés

FROG'S LEGS

8 pairs of small fresh frogs' legs
1½ cups buttermilk
1 tsp. Tabasco Green Pepper Sauce
1 cup flour
1 Tbsp. salt
¼ tsp. ground white pepper
¼ tsp. dried thyme
½ cup clarified butter (see recipe, this page)
1 clove garlic, crushed
1 tsp. red wine vinegar
2 lemons, halved, for garnish

PERSILLADE SAUCE

2 Tbsp. extra-virgin olive oil
6 cloves garlic, chopped
Leaves from 15 sprigs flat-leaf parsley, chopped
¼ tsp. salt

1. Rinse the frogs' legs, then place them in a food storage bag with the buttermilk and green pepper sauce, and let marinate in the refrigerator for 2 hours.

2. To make the persillade sauce: Heat the oil in a small saucepan over medium-low heat. Add the chopped garlic and parsley, and cook until the parsley is wilted and the garlic is fragrant. Remove from heat. Transfer the parsley mixture to a small food processor or blender. Add the ¼ teaspoon salt and puree. Transfer the mixture into one corner of a small plastic sandwich bag.

3. Combine the flour, 1 tablespoon salt, pepper, and thyme in a wide bowl. Shake the excess buttermilk off the frogs' legs and coat them lightly with the flour mixture.

4. Heat the clarified butter in a medium skillet over medium-high heat. Add the crushed garlic. When the butter is bubbling, add the frogs' legs and sauté until golden, turning once. Transfer the frogs' legs to paper towels to drain. Carefully add the vinegar to the skillet and whisk to make a sauce.

5. Arrange 2 frogs' legs on each of 4 plates. Spoon some of the butter sauce over the legs, trying to avoid picking up the solids on the bottom of the pan. With scissors, snip off the corner of the plastic bag with the parsley sauce. Squeeze out lines of the persillade across the frogs' legs. Garnish with lemon halves. SERVES FOUR.

Abita Springs Stuffed Quail

STUFFED QUAILS

¼ lb. andouille (see this page) or other smoked sausage
4 green onions, finely chopped
½ red bell pepper, diced
1 tsp. dried basil
1 cup jumbo lump crabmeat
1 cup shrimp, crab, or chicken stock (see recipe, this page)
2 cups bread crumbs
2 eggs, beaten separately
8 baby quails, rib and backbones removed
4 tsp. butter, softened

EGGPLANT

1 eggplant, at least 2½ inches in diameter, peeled and cut into ¼-inch-thick rounds
1 cup flour
1 Tbsp. salt-free Creole seasoning
1 Tbsp. salt
¼ cup milk
¼ cup extra-virgin olive oil

SAUCE

2 green onions, chopped
½ cup dry white wine
2 cups chicken stock
1 Tbsp. tomato paste
Pinch of dried sage
Pinch of dried thyme
Salt and freshly ground black pepper to taste

1. Preheat the oven to 400 degrees F. Cook the andouille, green onions, bell pepper, and basil in a large skillet over medium heat until the sausage is lightly browned. Pour off any excess fat.

2. Add the crabmeat and stock and bring to a boil. Gently stir to combine everything without breaking up the crab lumps. Over medium-high heat, reduce the liquid by about one-third.

3. Remove the skillet from the heat and stir in the bread crumbs to make a thick stuffing. Cool the stuffing in the refrigerator for 20 minutes. Then mix one of the eggs into the stuffing.

4. Fill each of the quails with some of the stuffing and arrange them in a roasting pan, breast side up. Dot each quail with ½ teaspoon of the butter. Roast until golden brown, 12–15 minutes. (If you have a convection oven, set it to convect.)

5. Meanwhile, cut each slice of eggplant into perfect circles with a 2-inch cookie or biscuit cutter and set aside. Combine the flour, Creole seasoning, and salt in a wide bowl. Whisk the milk and remaining egg together in another bowl. Dip eggplant rounds into the egg mixture, then into the flour mixture.

6. Heat the olive oil in a medium skillet over high heat and sauté the eggplant until golden brown on both sides. Drain the eggplant on paper towels and keep warm.

7. Transfer the roasted quail to a platter and keep warm. To make the sauce: Place the roasting pan over a burner on medium-high heat. Add the green onions and cook until they begin to brown. Add the wine and bring it to a boil, whisking to dissolve the crusty bits stuck to the bottom of the pan. Add the chicken stock, tomato paste, and herbs, and return to a boil. Reduce to about 1 cup. Season to taste with salt and pepper and strain the sauce through a fine sieve.

8. Spoon some of the sauce over each of 8 warmed dinner plates. Arrange a few eggplant rounds on the sauce and top with a stuffed quail. SERVES EIGHT.

Mirliton and Root Vegetable Gratin

2 slices lemon
2 whole cloves
1 tsp. black peppercorns
1 rutabaga, peeled and sliced into ¼-inch-thick slices
2 lb. carrots, peeled and cut on the bias into ¼-inch-thick coins
2 lb. parsnips, prepared the same way as the carrots (substitute turnips)
4 mirlitons, halved, seed removed, sliced ¼ inch thick
3 cloves garlic
1½ cups grated Gruyere cheese
1½ cups finely grated Parmesan cheese
1 tsp white pepper
Pinch nutmeg
1 pint whipping cream
2 egg yolks, beaten
1 cup bread crumbs

1. Preheat the oven to 400 degrees F.

2. Bring a large saucepan of water to a rolling boil with the lemon, cloves, and peppercorns. Add the rutabaga slices (it helps to do this in a large sieve or a chinoise), boil for about 2 minutes, then remove and drain. Repeat with the carrots, parsnips, and mirlitons. (The mirlitons will only require about 1 minute.)

3. Crush the garlic cloves and use them to wipe the inside of a 2-inch-deep, 12 by 9-inch glass baking dish. Discard what's left of the garlic.

4. Layer the vegetables in the baking dish in the order listed, sprinkling a mixture of the cheeses between the layers. Season with white pepper and (sparingly) nutmeg. The cheeses will provide all the salt this needs.

5. Combine the whipping cream and the egg yolks thoroughly. Pour the mixture over the vegetables. Cover with aluminum foil and bake for 1 hour.

6. Remove the foil, sprinkle bread crumbs in a thin layer over the top, and return to the oven. Continue baking, uncovered, until the crust browns.

7. Remove from the oven and allow to rest and cool for at least 10 minutes before serving. This is better warm than hot. MAKES ABOUT TWELVE SIDE PORTIONS

Broiled Mushrooms with Italian Sausage

4 links hot or sweet Italian sausage
¼ tsp. crushed red pepper
½ tsp. dried oregano
½ tsp. salt
10 sprigs flat-leaf parsley, leaves only, chopped
⅔ cup bread crumbs
1 lb. medium whole white mushrooms, stemmed
⅓ cup shredded Fontina or mozzarella cheese

1. Preheat the broiler. Remove the sausage from the casings. Place the sausage meat in a large skillet over medium heat and cook, breaking up the sausage with a kitchen fork until it begins to brown. Pour off any excess fat.

2. Add the crushed red pepper, oregano, salt, and ½ cup of water, and continue to cook until the sausage meat is no longer pink. Add the parsley and bread crumbs, and mix in well. Add a little more water, if needed, to keep the mixture from being very dry. (It should not be very wet, either.) Remove from the heat.

3. Slice off a sliver the size of a dime from the top of the mushroom cap to make a flat area. Stuff a heaping teaspoon of the sausage mixture into the cavity of each mushroom. Place the mushrooms, stuffing side up, on a baking pan. Place a generous pinch of the shredded cheese (as much as you can get to stay put) on top of the stuffing. Broil until the cheese melts and begins to brown. SERVES EIGHT TO TWELVE.

Boudin Blanc

3–4 yards of medium sausage casing

STOCK
4 chicken-leg quarters
1 small pork shoulder (Boston butt), about 3–4 lb.
1 large onion, cut into eighths
2 bay leaves
2 ribs celery, chopped Stems from
1 bunch of flat-leaf parsley
½ tsp. thyme
½ tsp. marjoram
1 tsp. black peppercorns

FILLING
4 slices bacon
1 lb. pork liver, cut into ½-inch-thick slices
1 medium onion, coarsely chopped
½ bell pepper, coarsely chopped
1 rib celery, coarsely chopped
1½ tsp. cayenne, plus more to taste
4½ tsp. salt, plus more to taste
3 cups uncooked short-grain rice (not parboiled or converted)
1 bunch of flat-leaf parsley, leaves only, finely chopped
2 bunches of green onions, green parts only, finely chopped
1 tsp. freshly ground black pepper

1. Unroll the sausage casing and soak it in cold water for an hour or so. Pull it open and run water through the casing for a few seconds. Keep moist.

2. Put all the stock ingredients into a large pot and add enough water to cover—at least a gallon (16 cups) of water. Bring to a light boil and cook, uncovered, for 2 hours. Skim the fat and foam off the surface as the stock cooks.

3. To make the filling: Fry the bacon in a large skillet until crisp. Remove the bacon and reserve for another use. Add the pork liver and all the other filling ingredients up to (but not including) the rice to the drippings, and sauté over medium heat until the liver is tender. Add ½ cup of the simmering stock and cook 10 minutes more. Transfer to a bowl, let cool, and then refrigerate.

4. Remove the chicken and pork from the stockpot and set aside. Strain the stock and discard the solids. Return the stock to a light boil and reduce to 2 quarts.

5. Reserve two of the chicken-leg quarters for another purpose. Skin and bone the other two and dice the meat. Dice the pork shoulder, cutting across the grain of the meat. Refrigerate all this when finished.

6. When the stock is reduced, pour 5 cups into a large saucepan. Add the rice, bring to a boil, then reduce heat and simmer, covered, about 25 minutes, or until the rice is very tender and borderline gummy. Fluff and set aside.

7. If you have a meat grinder, fit it with the coarse blade or ¼-inch die. Combine the diced chicken, pork, and liver, and run the mixture through the grinder once. If you don't have a grinder, use a food processor, but stop short of mincing the ingredients.

8. Combine the ground meat mixture with the rice, chopped parsley, green onions, and black pepper. Add 1–2 cups of the stock, a little at a time, and mix well. You've added enough stock when you can easily form the mixture into a ball that doesn't stick to your fingers. Add more cayenne and salt to taste.

9. At this point, you can either stuff the boudin into the casing, or you can make boudin balls without casing. Either way, microwave until quite warm inside before serving. MAKES ABOUT TWENTY-FOUR 4-INCH LINKS.

New Orleans Shrimp Spring Rolls

SHRIMP
Leafy tops from a bunch of celery
1 bay leaf
1 Tbsp. Tabasco
½ lemon, sliced 2 Tbsp. salt
1 lb. medium shrimp (25–30 count)

ROLLS
8 oz. rice stick noodles, soaked in cold water for about 45 minutes
12 round rice-paper wrappers
½ cup red rémoulade sauce (see Shrimp Rémoulade with Two Sauces,this page)

GARNISH
Asian-style chili-garlic sauce
2 green onions, finely chopped

1. To prepare the shrimp: Bring ½ gallon (8 cups) of water to a boil in a pot. Add all the ingredients up to (but not including) the shrimp. Boil the water for 5 minutes, then add the shrimp. Remove the pot from the heat immediately and allow the shrimp to steep for 4 minutes, or until the shell separates from the meat easily.

2. Drain shrimp in a colander and set aside until cool enough to handle. Peel and devein the shrimp.

3. Bring a small pot of water to a boil. After the noodles have soaked for about 45 mintues, drain them, then plunge them in the boiling water for about a minute. Drain again and let cool.

4. Brush the rice-paper wrappers with water and let them soften. When the rice paper is stretchy, lay about 3 tablespoons of the noodles in a line about two-thirds of the way down the rice paper. Drizzle about a tablespoon of the rémoulade sauce across the noodles. Place 4–6 shrimp on top of the noodles, then roll up the rice paper. When

the noodles and shrimp are covered, tuck in the loose ends of the rice paper and finish rolling.

5. Garnish rolls with squirts of the chili-garlic sauce and chopped green onions. MAKES TWELVE ROLLS.

Savory Waffles

1 cup self-rising flour
½ tsp. granulated onion
¼ tsp. dry dill
½ tsp. salt 3 Tbsp. extra-virgin olive oil or melted butter
1 egg, beaten
1 cup half-and-half

1. Preheat a waffle iron.

2. In a small bowl, mix all the dry ingredients.

3. In a larger bowl, whisk together all the wet ingredients.

4. Add the dry ingredients to the wet ingredients and whisk slowly until all the flour is wet. Don't eliminate all the lumps.

5. Pour about 3 tablespoons of the batter into the center of each half of the waffle iron, covering only one square completely and allowing the batter to flow into the surrounding squares. Close the cover and cook according to the manufacturer's instructions. The top of the waffle need not brown entirely.

6. Flip the waffle over, browned side up, and fill the center square with sour cream, soft-scrambled eggs, crabmeat with hollandaise, or whatever else you might think of. MAKES ABOUT A DOZEN WAFFLES.

Cauliflower and Endive Gratin

Servings: 4-6 dishes

Ingredients:

1/2 head cauliflower, cut into florets

2 heads endives, cut into smaller pieces

1 teaspoon dried oregano

1/2 cup coconut milk

1 pinch nutmeg

Salt, pepper to taste

Directions:

1. Mix the cauliflower with the endives, oregano, coconut milk, nutmeg, salt and pepper in a bowl then transfer the vegetables to a baking tray lined with baking paper.

2. Drizzle with olive oil and bake in a preheated oven at 350F for 30-40 minutes or until tender and golden brown. Serve right away.

Spicy Hummus

Servings: 4-6 dishes

Ingredients:

2 cups canned garbanzo beans, drained

1/4 cup walnuts

14 cup pine nuts

2 garlic cloves

1/4 cup hot water

1/4 cup extra virgin olive oil

1/2 teaspoon chili flakes

Salt, pepper

Directions:

1. Combine all the ingredients together in a blender or food processor and mix until smooth and creamy.

2. Adjust the taste with salt and pepper and spoon the mixture into a serving bowl.

3. Drizzle with olive oil and sprinkle with freshly ground black pepper before serving.

4. Serve with tortilla chips or toasted bread slices.

Herb Brussels Sprouts

Servings: 4-6 dishes

Ingredients:

30 Brussels sprouts

4 tablespoons olive oil

1/2 cup chopped parsley

2 tablespoons chopped oregano

2 garlic cloves, minced

Salt, pepper

Directions:

1. Wash the Brussels sprouts well then cut them into quarters. Set aside.

2. Heat the olive oil in a heavy skillet and stir in the garlic. Sauce only for 30 seconds, then add the sprouts.

3. Turn the heat on low and cook, stirring often, for 10-15 minutes or until tender. Remove from heat, add salt and pepper and stir in the chopped herbs.

4. Serve immediately while still warm.

Roasted Squash Salad

Servings: 6-8 dishes

Ingredients:

1 pound winter squash, cubed
1/4 cup olive oil
2 celery stalks, sliced
1/2 cup walnuts, coarsely chopped
1 tablespoon Dijon mustard
1 tablespoon apple cider
2 tablespoons olive oil
Salt, pepper

Directions:

1. Mix the squash cubes with 1/4 cup olive oil in a baking tray lined with baking paper.

2. Sprinkle with salt and pepper and bake in a preheated oven at 375F for 20-30 minutes or until tender and slightly caramelized.

3. Remove from oven and transfer to a bowl. Stir in the celery and walnuts. To make the dressing, mix the mustard with apple cider and olive oil.

4. Gently mix it with the vegetables in the bowl. Serve the salad fresh.

Exotic Rice

Servings: 6-8 dishes

Ingredients:

3 cups cooked rice
1/4 cup olive oil
1/4 cup pineapple juice
1 cup pineapple, cubed
2 cups arugula leaves
1 teaspoon fresh ginger
2 green onions, sliced
1 cup walnuts, coarsely chopped
4 oz tofu, cut into bite size pieces and fried
Salt, pepper

Directions:

1. Place the rice in a bowl and stir in the pineapple cubes, green onions, walnuts, tofu and arugula leaves.

2. In a small bowl, mix the pineapple juice with the ginger, olive oil, salt and pepper.

3. Pour this dressing over the rice and mix gently.

4. Serve the rice as a side dish or main dish if you prefer.

Sweet Potato Falafel

Servings: 4-6 dishes

Ingredients:

2 sweet potatoes
1/2 teaspoon cumin powder
2 garlic cloves, minced
4 tablespoons chopped cilantro
1 tablespoon lemon juice
1/2 cup sesame seeds
Salt, pepper

Directions:

1. Wrap the sweet potatoes in tin foil and bake them in the oven for 30 minutes.

2. Scoop the flesh into a bowl and mash it with a fork. Add the cumin powder, garlic, cilantro and lemon juice. Season with salt and pepper.

3. Wet your hands and form small balls of mixture. Roll each ball into sesame seeds and arrange them all on a baking tray lined with baking paper.

4. Bake in a preheated oven at 375F for 10-20 minutes or until golden brown. Serve warm or

Stuffed Mushrooms

Servings: 6 dishes

Ingredients:

12 medium size mushrooms (Champignon)
2 oz firm tofu, crumbled
2 oz silken tofu
1 green onion, chopped
1/4 celery stalk, finely chopped
2 tablespoons ground walnuts
Salt, pepper

Directions:

1. In a bowl, mix the crumbled tofu with the silken tofu, green onion, celery, walnuts, salt and pepper.

2. Spoon this mixture into each of the 12 mushrooms and arrange them all on a baking tray lined with baking paper.

3. Bake in a preheated oven at 350F for 30 minutes. Serve warm or cold.

Grilled Marinated Zucchini

Servings: 4-6 dishes

Ingredients:

2 medium size zucchini, sliced lengthwise
4 tablespoons olive oil
Salt, pepper
2 tablespoons balsamic vinegar
2 tablespoons apple cider
2 tablespoons chopped parsley

Directions:

1. Sprinkle the zucchini slices with salt and pepper and brush them with olive oil.

2. Heat a grill pan and cook the zucchini slices on both sides until tender.

3. Remove from heat into a bowl and set aside, covered with a lid.

4. Mix the balsamic vinegar with the apple cider and chopped parsley. If you want, you can also add 1 garlic clove, minced. Pour this dressing over the warm zucchinis and let them marinade for 30 minutes at least.

Broccoli Crunchy Salad

Servings: 4-6 dishes

Ingredients:

4 cups broccoli florets
2 tablespoons lemon juice
1 teaspoon dates syrup
2 tablespoons olive oil
2 crisp apples, cored and sliced
1 red onion, sliced
1 cup walnuts, coarsely chopped
2 shallots + 2 tablespoons olive oil
Salt, pepper to taste

Directions:

1. Place the broccoli florets in a steamer and cook until tender, 15-20 minutes. When done, transfer the florets to a bowl.

2. Gently stir in the lemon juice mixed with dates syrup, salt, pepper and olive oil. Transfer to a large serving plate.

3. Top with the apple slices and set aside.

4. Heat the olive oil in a skillet and stir in the shallots.

5. Sauté for 10 minutes or more until crisp.

6. Scatter the shallots over the broccoli and top with walnut pieces. Serve immediately.

Tofu, Celery and Cilantro Salad

Servings: 4-6 dishes

Ingredients:

8 oz tofu, cut into strips
2 celery stalks, sliced
1/2 cup fresh cilantro, chopped
2 green onions, chopped
2 tomatoes, chopped
1 1/2 cups cooked quinoa
1 red bell pepper, cored and sliced
1/2 teaspoon cumin powder
2 tablespoons olive oil
Salt, pepper

Directions:

1. Heat the olive oil in a skillet. Sprinkle the tofu with cumin powder and fry it in the hot oil until slightly golden brown.

2. In a bowl, mix the tofu with the celery, cilantro, green onions, tomatoes, quinoa and bell pepper.

3. Adjust the taste with salt and pepper and serve as a side dish or as a main dish.

Tomato Cobbler

Servings: 4-6 dishes

Ingredients:

5 ripe tomatoes, peeled and cubed, drained of juices
1 tablespoon cornstarch
Salt, pepper
1 cup all purpose flour
1 cup whole wheat flour
1/2 cup coconut oil
1/2 teaspoon baking soda
1/2 cup applesauce
1 teaspoon dried thyme

Directions:

1. Mix the tomatoes with the cornstarch, salt, pepper and dried thyme and transfer to a deep dish baking pan.

2. In a bowl, combine the flours with a pinch of salt, baking soda, coconut oil and applesauce. Mix well then spoon the batter over the tomatoes in the pan.

3. Bake in a preheated oven at 350F for 40 minutes or until golden brown and fragrant.

4. Serve warm or chilled.

Apple and Cranberry Chutney

Servings: 4-8 dishes

Ingredients:

2 pounds apples, peeled, cored and diced
3 large onion, chopped
1 tablespoon fresh grated ginger
1/2 teaspoon chili flakes
1 cup sugar
1 cup cider vinegar
2 cups cranberries
Salt, pepper

Directions:

1. Mix the apples with the onion, ginger, chili flakes, sugar, vinegar, salt and pepper in a heavy saucepan and cook for 20 minutes.

2. Add the cranberries and cook for another 10 minutes. If you're not going to serve it right away, pour it into clean jars and seal with a lid. You can preserve it this way for a few months.

Roasted Tomato Salsa

Servings: 6-8 dishes

Ingredients:

5 Roma tomatoes, cut in quarters
1 red onion, cut in wedges
2 garlic cloves
4 tablespoons olive oil
1 chili pepper, seeded and sliced
1/2 cup coriander leaves, chopped
1/4 cup parsley leaves, chopped
Salt, pepper

Directions:

1. Place the tomatoes and red onion in a baking tray. Add a bit of salt and pepper and drizzle with olive oil.

2. Bake in a preheated oven at 375F for 25 minutes or until slightly caramelized. Remove from oven and let the vegetables cool.

3. Chop them coarsely and place them in a bowl, adding the chili pepper, coriander leaves and parsley leaves.

4. Mix gently and serve with your favorite dishes.

Red Onion and Rosemary Focaccia

Servings: 6-8 dishes

Ingredients:

4 cups all purpose flour
1 teaspoon instant yeast
1 1/2 cups warm water
1 tablespoon sugar
1 teaspoon salt
1/2 cup olive oil
1 large red onion, cut into rings
2 tablespoons fresh rosemary, chopped

Directions:

1. In a bowl, mix the warm water with the yeast and let it bloom for 10 minutes. Stir in the sugar then add the flour and salt. \

2. Knead the dough for at least 15 minutes or until elastic and easy to work with. Cover the bowl with plastic wrap and let it rise for 1 hour in a warm place.

3. When risen enough, roll the dough into a 1/2-inch thick sheet and transfer it to a baking tray. Using your fingertips, make indentations on the surface of the dough then drizzle with olive oil. Scatter the red onion rings and sprinkle with chopped rosemary.

4. Bake in a preheated oven at 375F for 20-30 minutes or until fluffy and golden brown on the edges. Serve it cut into strips.

Tofu Croquettes with Cranberry Sauce

Servings: 4 dishes

Ingredients:

Croquettes:
4 thick tofu slices
1 teaspoon mixed herbs
1 shallot
2 tablespoons coriander leaves
2 tablespoons sesame seeds
2 tablespoons breadcrumbs
Sauce:
1 1/2 cups cranberries
1 tablespoon apple vinegar
1 teaspoon dates syrup
Salt, pepper

Directions:

1. Place the ingredients for the croquettes in a food processor and pulse until it comes together like dough. Form small croquettes and fry them in hot coconut oil until golden brown. Set aside.

2. To make the sauce, mix the cranberries with the vinegar, dates syrup, salt and pepper and cook until soft and easy to mash. Using a fork, mash it slightly then serve the croquettes dipped into this sauce.

Lemon Grilled Asparagus

Servings: 4

Ingredients:

1 bunch asparagus, trimmed
juice from 1/2 lemon
1 tablespoon lemon zest
4 tablespoons olive oil
Salt, pepper

Directions:

1. In a bowl, mix the lemon juice with the lemon zest, olive oil, salt and pepper.

2. Brush the asparagus spears with the mixture you made earlier then heat a grill pan on medium heat.

3. Grill the asparagus until tender and serve immediately, drizzled with the leftover dressing.

You've reached the end of this edition of the series of the book, eating like a boss yet? Check out the second edition of this book for even more recipes and have your taste buds in heaven.

Thank you for purchasing this book, for more books please visit

www.dorvilpublishing.com

29234639R00047

Made in the USA
Middletown, DE
21 December 2018